To:

From:

Date:

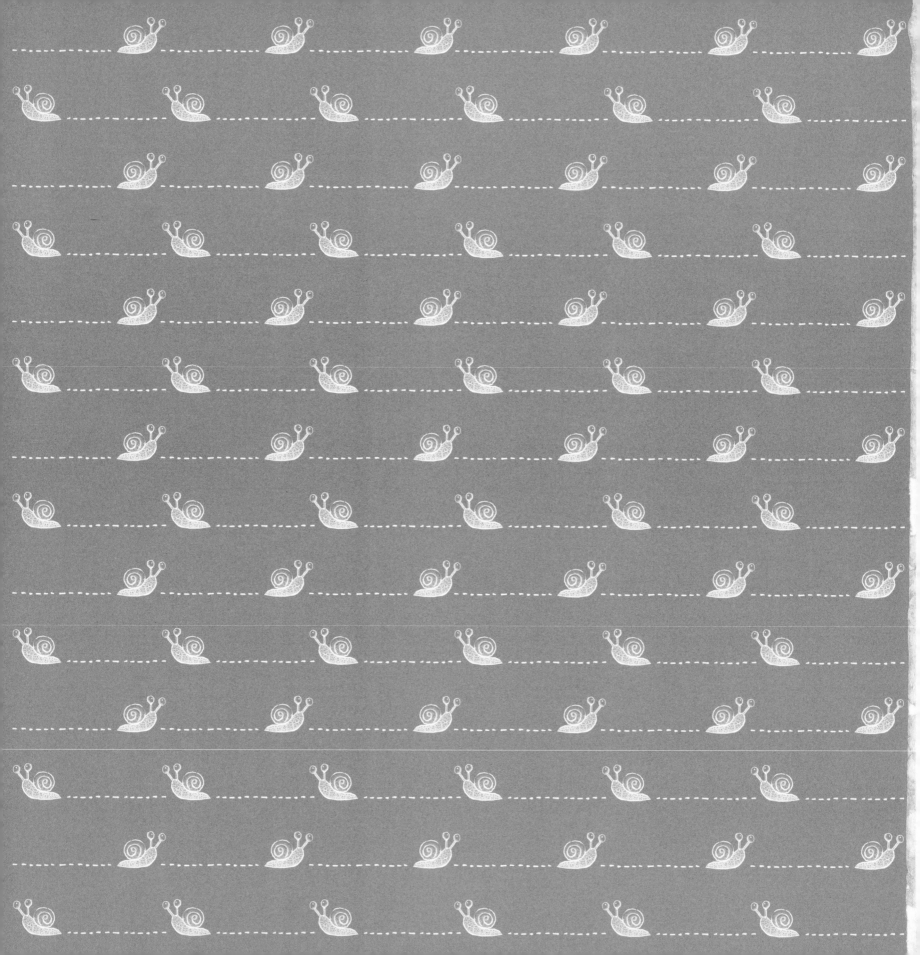

ONLY YOU CAN BE YOU!

What Makes You Different Makes You GREAT

Nathan and Sally CLARKSON

illustrated by Tim WARNES

Tommy NELSON

An Imprint of Thomas Nelson

Published in Nashville, Tennessee, by Tommy Nelson. Tommy Nelson is an imprint of Thomas Nelson. Thomas Nelson is a registered trademark of HarperCollins Christian Publishing, Inc.

Front cover banner pattern by Janine Vangool, *UPPERCASE* magazine.

Tommy Nelson titles may be purchased in bulk for educational, business, fund-raising, or sales promotional use. For information, please email SpecialMarkets@ThomasNelson.com.

Library of Congress Cataloging-in-Publication Data

Names: Clarkson, Sally, author. | Clarkson, Nathan, author. | Warnes, Tim, illustrator.
Title: Only you can be you / Sally Clarkson and Nathan Clarkson ; illustrated by Tim Warnes.
Description: Tommy Nelson, Nashville, Tennessee, USA : Tommy Nelson, [2019] | Includes bibliographical references and index.
Identifiers: LCCN 2019013078| ISBN 9781400211432 (hardcover : alk. paper) | ISBN 9781400211449 (board book : alk. paper) | ISBN 9781400211463 (e-book : alk. paper)
Subjects: LCSH: Identity (Psychology)--Religious aspects--Christianity--Juvenile literature. | Board books.
Classification: LCC BV4509.5 .C54 2019 | DDC 242/.62--dc23 LC record available at https://urldefense.proofpoint.com/v2/url?u=https-3A__lccn.loc .gov_2019013078&d=DwIFAg&c=hh7v4vz1gCZ__1Ci-hUEVZfsSwlOcPhT2q 8Zs1ka6Ao&r=iJLvdNeAqBGDHudUu-kBcE-z6kmidKLKPuYAara8KTY&m=2Rc on9cuEaCYxIWZahXQ0ZKCM4Mu7DjU1XWfNpJbYZU&s=Jo _p4aqgQfY7vB_pJd1zVn4peZha4kdKjuMXeKAngoM&e=

Printed in China

21 22 23 DSC 6 5 4 3 2

Mfr: DSC / Dongguan, China / July 2021 / PO #12088303

To wonderful Nathan, who taught me to lean into the adventure of life, to value differences as beautiful by design, and to love well every day

—Sally

To my mom, who was the first to show me how beautiful it is to be the completely special, unique, and different person God designed me to be

—Nathan

For Heidi (small and smiley!)

—Tim

Everyone's different,
and that's okay.

The Maker of everything

made us that way.

Maybe you're LOUD
and are bursting with life,

Or maybe you're quiet
and seem kind of shy.

Maybe you're tall
and can almost touch clouds,

Or maybe you're short
and can dart through the crowds.

Maybe you're playful,
artistic, and free,

Or maybe you're **organized**,
tidy, and clean.

Maybe you love
to play tag with your friends,

Or maybe you create your own world of pretend.

Maybe you're BRAVE.

You're the king of the hill!

Or maybe you hide
and can be very still.

Maybe you're **TOUGH**
with big muscles and might,

Or maybe you're tender
and let yourself cry.

Maybe you **BUILD** forts

with sheets

hung on trees,

Or maybe you dream of the stories you read.

Maybe with blocks you build towers so tall,

Or maybe you make clever gadgets for all.

Maybe you're f**u**n**n**y
and tell silly jokes,

Or maybe you're wishful
and share all your hopes.

Maybe you're **FAST**
and can win every race,

Or maybe you're measured
and keep a set pace.

Maybe you're handy—
with tools you're a pro!

Or maybe you plant seeds
to help gardens grow.

Maybe you're **dark**,
or maybe you're light.

Maybe you're **BIG**,
or maybe you're slight.

Each person's unique.
Only **you can** be you!

You're *perfectly different*—
no other will do.

Everyone's different,
and that's okay.

The **Maker of everything**

made us that way.